Sue Lawrence is known throughout Britain and beyond as a food writer and journalist. In addition to regular appearan
since she won BBC's
has also w
baking, i
The Sue L
In (2011)
Scottish Be

Chicken Stock
Soup
Red Lentils

The *Scottish Soup* Bible

Sue Lawrence

Illustrated by Bob Dewar

BIRLINN

First published in 2017 by
Birlinn Limited
West Newington House
10 Newington Road
Edinburgh
EH9 1QS

www.birlinn.co.uk

2

ISBN: 978 1 78027 484 3

British Library Cataloguing-in-Publication Data
A catalogue record for this book is available
from the British Library

Designed and typeset by Mark Blackadder

Printed and bound by Bell & Bain Ltd, Glasgow

Contents

Introduction

Soup is something we have always done well in Scotland. Since the first soup pot was hung over a peat fire, we have chopped and stirred, simmered and supped. Local produce – fish, shellfish, fish bones, mutton, lamb or beef bones, barley, root vegetables, seaweed, nettles and kail – have been thrown into the pot with water and cooked to nourishing perfection.

Well-known soups such as Scotch Broth, Cock-a-Leekie and Cullen Skink need little introduction. There have been recipes for these, with many regional variations, in historical cookbooks over the centuries. And let us not forget that wonderful coastal crab and rice-based soup Partan Bree, Shetland's memorable Reestit Mutton Soup and Bawd Bree, that magnificent hare soup flavoured with thyme and port. All these can be meals in themselves, served in large bowls with bread, bannocks or oatcakes on the side.

Alternatively they can be served in shallow soup plates as a starter before the main course: which is how I ate soup as a child every single day, come rain, hail or shine. Yes, even in the heatwaves of nostalgic childhood summers, there was always hot soup to come home to. It was part of growing up in Scotland. Nothing fancy – my mum's soups were lentil, split-pea, tattie or broth – but the soup pot was always there, bubbling away. It was a kitchen fixture, like a toaster or a kettle. The soup pot sat on the stove in every season (this was pre-central heating, remember!); it was an indication that all was well in the Scots kitchen.

Sometimes, if unexpected visitors arrived, more would be added to the pot. And that's the wonderful thing about soup: it can be eked out with even more nourishing ingredients to feed more mouths if necessary. The soup pot

is a symbol of sharing, of sitting round a table together, soup spoons in hand.

As children, when we were ill, a mug of soup was always first on the sick-bed menu. Ironically, it was the only time my mum would ever buy tinned soup, as I used to beg for tinned tomato soup. So she would give way, even though it did no good at all for the ill child, with its overpowering sweetness. After day two, therefore, it was back to the restorative powers of home-made! It is surely no coincidence that when we are unwell or just a little under the weather, our bodies crave soup. Hearty vegetable soup, wholesome lentil soup or perhaps a light chicken broth – all slip down easily while nourishing the body and soothing the soul. In the comfort food stakes, in my opinion you can forget bangers and mash or jam roly-poly. Give me a good bowl of soup any day; though nowadays I often add some very unScottish ingredients, such as root ginger, garlic or fresh chilli to aid its healing properties.

Some references suggest that Scots' soup-making skills can be attributed to the French influence of the Auld Alliance from many centuries ago. And whereas certain soups and potages seem to be directly linked to this, it is a fact that long before the claret trade began with Leith and long before Mary Queen of Scots sailed from France to take her throne in Scotland, we were ladling out tasty soups. They were undoubtedly not grand, complicated or sophisticated, but rather, they were homely, hearty and nourishing. Which is my idea of perfection in a soup bowl, whether I am feeling well or not so well.

In the kitchens of the past couple of centuries, above the range would be a swee, a moveable hook, and from that hung a soup pot. In older days, in the Highlands and Islands, the pot would have been three-legged and would have stood over the peat fire. The soup pot, filled with wholesome nutritious broth or soup, was the one kitchen item – as well as the iron girdle to bake bannocks and oatcakes on – that was ubiquitous throughout the land.

Old recipes contained many ingredients which are less acceptable to the modern palate, such as ox, calf or sheep's heads, ox heel, cockerel, eels. I do not feel that in omitting these I am ignoring history, just being practical. Often the animal head was used to add flavour but this is easily replicated by using instead home-made stock from roast chicken, beef or lamb – or good quality, preferably organic, stock cubes.

Soup and baking have always been our specialities in Scotland, perhaps because they are both comforting foods; but they also go so well together. In the poor households of Scotland's past, a plate of soup would have been the main meal accompanied by something home-baked – a beremeal bannock on Orkney, an oatcake in the Highlands, a tattie scone in the Borders – and this constituted the ideal meal, from both a nutritional and also an emotional point of view. Forget all this obsession with Scandinavian Hygge; let's hear it for the restorative, comforting and health-giving qualities of Scotland's soup.

Fish and Seafood

Cullen Skink (Traditional)

The classic Cullen Skink is made with Finnan haddock (Finnan haddie) which is a whole haddock that has the head removed but the bone left in. It is then split (so the bone is left down one side) then brined and cold-smoked. It is wonderful simply grilled with a knob of butter for either breakfast or tea. Though not as widely available as smoked haddock fillets, Finnan haddock can usually be ordered from good fishmongers a day or two in advance.

The Finnan haddock is named after the village of Findon, south of Aberdeen, where the cure was perfected. Cullen is a fishing village on the Moray Coast to the north east of Aberdeen and is now famous for its soup. Skink is the old Scots word for shin and was the name of a traditional soup made using a shin of beef. When made in a fishing village, however, an accessible local ingredient – haddock – was used instead. And lo, Cullen Skink was born!

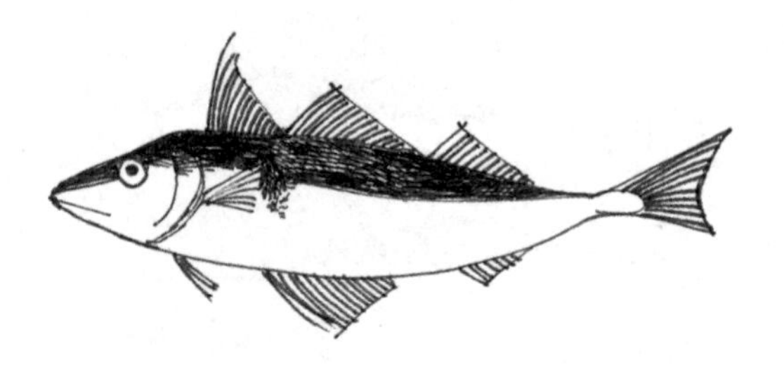

Serves 4–6

2 Finnan haddock
2 medium onions, peeled and finely chopped
500g floury potatoes (unpeeled weight), peeled and chopped into dice
200ml full-fat milk
40g unsalted butter
Chopped chives, to serve

Place the haddock in a large pan with 400ml cold water. Bring slowly to the boil, then simmer for 6–8 minutes until the fish is just cooked. Cover tightly and leave for about 10 minutes.

Remove the fish with a slotted spoon and flake into large chunks, discarding the bones and skin. Set the fish aside.

Add the onions and potatoes to the pan with the milk and plenty of pepper (no salt). Cover and cook over a moderate heat for 12–15 minutes until the vegetables are tender. Watch carefully as the milk tends to boil up rapidly.

Remove the pan from the heat and, using a potato masher, roughly mash the contents, keeping some of the texture. Add the fish followed by the butter, bring to the boil and then remove from the heat.

Season to taste and serve in warm bowls with some chopped chives.

Cullen Skink (with Smoked Haddock Fillets)

This is a modern version of Cullen Skink that is easier, as smoked haddock fillets are ubiquitous, whereas Finnan haddock often needs to be ordered.

Be sure to use floury potatoes, such as Maris Piper or King Edward, as they mash down to thicken the soup; waxy potatoes do not mash down as well.

When buying smoked haddock fillets, I insist on undyed. Even though in Scotland smoked haddock fillets used to be called 'yellow fish', the colour adds absolutely nothing. Always opt for a traditional smoke.

Serves 4–6

600g undyed smoked haddock fillets (3 good-sized fillets)
2 medium onions, peeled and finely chopped
500g floury potatoes (unpeeled weight), peeled and chopped into dice
200ml full-fat milk
40g unsalted butter or 200ml double cream
Chopped chives, to serve

Place the haddock in a large pan with 400ml cold water. Bring slowly to the boil then simmer for 3–4 minutes until the fish is just cooked. Then cover tightly and leave for about 10 minutes.

Remove the fish with a slotted spoon and flake into large chunks. Set the fish aside.

Add the onions and potatoes to the pan with the milk and plenty of pepper (no salt). Cover and cook over a moderate heat for 12–15 minutes until the vegetables are tender. Watch carefully as the milk tends to boil up rapidly.

Remove the pan from the heat and, using a potato masher, roughly mash the contents, keeping some of the texture. Add the fish followed by the butter, bring to the boil and then remove from the heat. (Or add the cream and simmer for a couple of minutes till warmed through.)

Season to taste and serve in a warm bowl with some chopped chives.

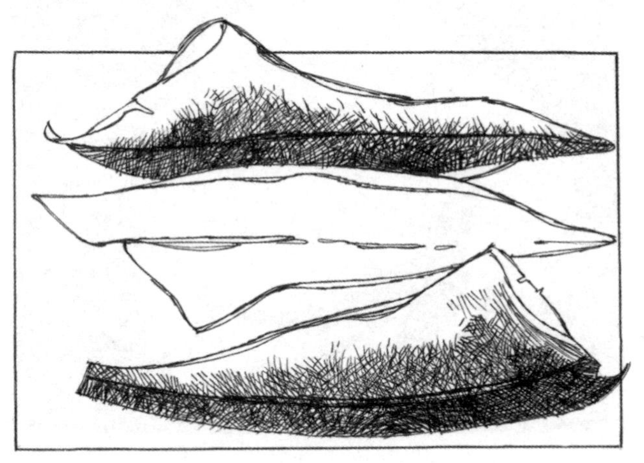

Partan Bree

This is a rich, creamy crab soup: partan means crab, bree means liquid or gravy. If you can, use a large live crab as your base: boil it for 15–20 minutes, then remove the creamy brown (body) meat to one bowl and the sweet white (claw and leg) meat to another. Discard the feathery 'dead men's fingers' as you work. Otherwise, fresh or defrosted frozen crabmeat will do.

Typical in many seaside areas of Scotland, this recipe has of course variations. Lady Clark of Tillypronie, in her 1909 cookery book, suggests adding some anchovy (presumably anchovy essence); I also rather like a shake or two of Worcestershire sauce. I have added a blade of mace for extra flavour.

Serve drizzled with a little extra cream if you like.

Serves 4

75g long-grain rice
600ml full-fat milk
A blade of mace
The meat of 1 large crab or about 300g fresh or defrosted frozen crabmeat – about 200g brown meat and 100g white meat
600ml fish stock, hot
150ml double cream plus extra cream to drizzle, optional
Anchovy essence

Cook the rice in the milk with the mace for about 15–20 minutes until tender, then discard the mace and tip the mixture into a liquidiser or food processor with the brown meat. Process until combined and tip back into the pan with the hot stock.

Reheat over a medium heat until just below boiling point, then add the white meat and the cream. Reheat gently for a couple of minutes and add salt, pepper and anchovy essence to taste. Serve in warm bowls and add an extra dash of anchovy essence – and extra cream – if you like.

Fishermen's Soup

This recipe was given to me by Arbroath fisherman Alec Smith, who went to sea for periods of some 4 to 5 days to catch mainly haddock and whiting. During the time at sea, there was plenty fish on board and so an old family recipe came into its own. This Fishermen's Soup is made one day then reheated the next. The quantities are quite large, but it is more main meal than first course.

The addition of evaporated milk might seem rather bizarre, but that is what the fishermen used to take to sea instead of fresh milk to put in their tea. If you do not approve, use double cream instead. Bizarrely I like the flavour of evaporated milk in this soup; it must take me back to my 1960s childhood when evaporated milk was used in everything from chicken *vol au vents* and Gypsy Tart to that definitive childhood treat, Jelly Whip (aka Jelly Fluff). An acquired taste, however, so double cream is a fine alternative.

Serves 6

2 large onions, peeled and chopped
6 medium potatoes, peeled and chopped into large chunks
2 heaped tablespoons medium oatmeal
6 thick fillets of haddock (about 1.5kg), each cut into about 8 large chunks
300ml evaporated milk or 150ml carton double cream
Freshly chopped parsley and thick oatcakes, to serve

Place the onions, potatoes and oatmeal in a very large saucepan with 2.25 litres cold water. Add 2 teaspoons of salt and plenty of freshly ground pepper. Bring to the boil, skimming off any scum. Once it is bubbling, add the fish, cover and lower to a simmer. Cook for 10 minutes, or just until the potatoes are tender. Remove from the heat and allow to cool completely before refrigerating or keeping somewhere cold.

Next day, reheat until hot, stir in the milk or cream and check the seasoning. Ladle into warm bowls, sprinkle over some parsley, crumble over some oatcakes and serve at once.

CO-OP

Winkle Soup

Making winkle soup is not for the faint-hearted. If you try not to think of them as sea snails, it might make it easier! The only other impediment then might be the time it takes to poke out the flesh from these tiny molluscs. This is the time to enlist help . . .

My recipe is based on an old Hebridean one in F. Marian McNeill's 1929 cookery book *The Scots Kitchen*. She stipulates gathering winkles on the rocks at low tide; I have a feeling most of us would prefer to collect them from the fishmonger, but foragers will be fortunate if they harvest a bucketful of winkles for this tasty soup. The texture is more like that of a brose, as it is thickened with oatmeal.

Whether you buy or forage, the winkles will need thorough cleaning. Give them many rinses under a running tap; these little molluscs collect a lot of sand.

Serves 2–3

Approx. 700–800g winkles
1 leek, thinly sliced
3 sticks celery, finely chopped
A few black peppercorns
Approx. 50g fine or medium oatmeal
A good handful of chives, chopped

Wash the winkles in a sieve under the tap, rinsing over and over until you can no longer see bits of sand or debris. Soak them in cold lightly salted water for 20–30 minutes, then rinse thoroughly again.

Place the leeks, celery and peppercorns in a pan with 750ml cold water and bring slowly to the boil. Tip in the winkles and bring back to the boil. Boil for 3 minutes, remove from the heat and strain over another pan. Let the winkles become cool then, using a long pin or thin skewer, poke out the flesh. First to come out of the opening of the shell is the dark 'foot' (a tiny dark brown cap), so discard that and retain the long body.

Meanwhile, reheat the liquor in the pan, and once you have a rolling boil, add the oatmeal in a slow, steady stream, stirring all the time so it does not get lumpy. I like to use a spurtle for this part, as it is not dissimilar to porridge-making!

You need enough oatmeal to make a thin gruel-like consistency: about 50g should do it. Cook, stirring, for about 15 minutes until thickened, then add the winkles back in. Reheat gently and add salt and pepper to taste before serving in warm bowls and scattering with chives.

Seafood Soup

This soup is not dissimilar to one of those chowders served on the east coast of the USA, often with crushed crackers on top. I like to serve this with crumbled oatcakes over the top. It can be made with whatever seafood there is available, but a combination of shellfish and white fish is good.

Serves 4

25g butter
1 leek, cleaned and finely chopped
1 large onion, peeled and finely chopped
2 large potatoes, peeled and cubed
600ml full-fat milk
600ml fish stock
400g mussels, well scrubbed (discard any open ones)
Approx. 3 heaped tablespoons of mashed potatoes (made from floury potatoes)
500g fillets of haddock, pollack or ling, cut into chunks
150ml double cream
Thick oatcakes, to serve
1 tablespoon freshly chopped parsley

Melt the butter in a pan and sweat the leek, onion and potatoes for about 10 minutes.

Meanwhile, warm the milk to tepid, then add to the pan with the fish stock. Add the mussels, bring to the boil, cover and simmer for about 3 minutes or until the mussels are opened. Remove the mussels with a slotted spoon and take the meat out of the shells. Set aside, discarding any that have remained closed, along with the shells.

Add the mashed potatoes, stir well to thicken, then add the fish chunks and the double cream. Bring to a simmer and cook gently for 3–4 minutes or until the fish is just cooked. Return the mussel meat to the pan and check the seasoning.

Serve in warm bowls with broken-up pieces of oatcakes sprinkled over the top. Top with parsley and serve at once.

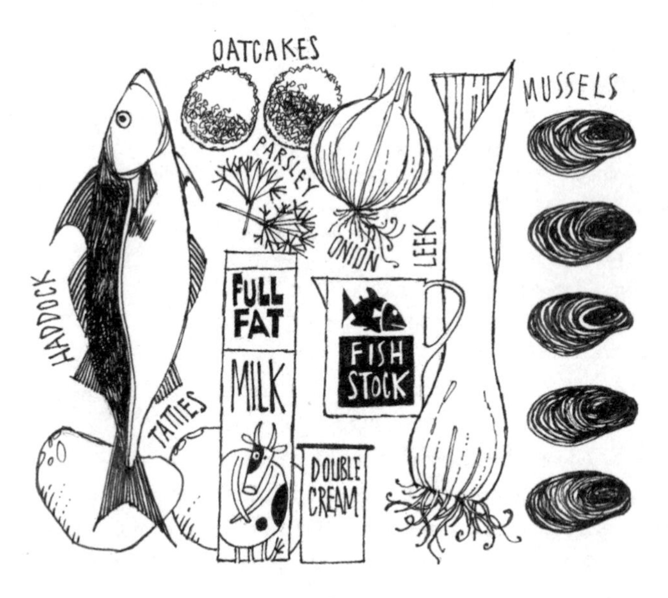

Salmon Soup

Traditionally, Salmon Soup would have been made in areas where wild salmon were fished. Though my recipe is more geared for modern days and uses salmon fillets, traditional recipes would have used perhaps only the head of the salmon, what flesh could be scraped away from the bones. Nothing was wasted; it is not by chance that we Scots have the reputation of being frugal.

Serves 3–4

400g potatoes (peeled weight), peeled and diced
700ml fish stock
1 large leek, cleaned and thinly sliced
8–10 black peppercorns
300g fresh salmon, skinned (tail-end fillet is fine)
200ml double cream
20g fresh chives, snipped

Place the potatoes and stock in a saucepan and bring to the boil. Cook for about 10 minutes or until the potatoes are almost – but not quite – tender. Add the leeks and peppercorns (no salt yet). Stir, then cut the salmon into large chunks and place these on top. Cover and simmer for about 10 minutes over a low heat until the fish is just cooked. Add salt to taste, then gently stir in the cream, taking great care not to break up the fish. Reheat for a minute or so and stir in the chives. Taste again to check seasoning before serving in warm bowls.

Arbroath Smokie and Lovage Soup

The Arbroath smokie was first recorded in history in Arbroath Abbey's land register in 1178, as a gift from King William to the monks. Because the village where they were originally made – Auchmithie, three miles north of Arbroath – has been dated back to when it was a Pictish settlement, the origin of the humble smokie probably goes back a good deal further. It was only in the 1880s when fishermen from Auchmithie were enticed to migrate to Arbroath and its new harbour that the fisherfolk moved, taking with them the secret of their uniquely smoked haddock.

A hot-smoked haddock, the smokie is gutted, beheaded, lightly brined and smoked until just cooked. It used to be the case in Auchmithie – and later in Arbroath – that smoke barrels were sunk into the gardens, the rim being about a foot or so above the ground. Pairs of whole, headless, gutted haddock were salted, tied by the tails and hung on wooden poles over smouldering beech or oak chips, then damp hessian bags were placed over the top. Depending on the size of the fish, they would need only 30–45 minutes' smoking time before emerging a gorgeous, bronzed, tarry colour with soft, succulent and delicately flavoured flesh. These days, the smoking is done in more or less the same way, but usually by commercial companies on a larger scale.

We are, however, fortunate in Scotland to have passionate producers such as Iain Spink, scion of the Arbroath Spink family who have been associated with smokies for decades. Iain gives craft demonstrations at farmers' markets round Scotland and still produces the most exquisite product in the traditional way.

Lovage was used in many old recipes in Scotland.

The flavour is, to my mind, a combination of citrus and celery, so if you cannot find it, add a couple of sticks of celery as you make the soup and then add a squeeze of lemon at the end.

Serves 4

1 pair of Arbroath smokies
50g lovage stalks and leaves and a handful of lovage leaves, chopped, to finish
1 medium onion, peeled and chopped
2 leeks, cleaned and sliced
500g potatoes (peeled weight), peeled and cubed
150ml double cream

Gently heat the smokies in a low oven for 10 minutes, then remove the flesh, taking great care to avoid the tiny creamy coloured bones.

Reserve the flesh and place the rest – skins and bones – in a pan. Add the 50g of lovage stalks and leaves and cover with 1.2 litres of cold water. Bring to the boil, then cover and simmer for 30 minutes.

Strain the liquid into a clean pan and add the onion, leek and potatoes. Bring to the boil and simmer for 15–20 minutes until the vegetables are tender.

Now liquidise in a liquidiser with the reserved flesh and the remaining chopped lovage leaves. Check the seasoning (you probably won't need to add much salt), then tip into a pan with the cream. Reheat gently without boiling and serve in warm bowls.

Mussel Brose

This is a delicious soup for a bitterly cold winter's day. Mussels are cooked lightly, the liquor is reheated with some milk and fish stock and then thickened with oatmeal: hence the name brose. Brose is traditionally made in the mornings instead of porridge in certain regions of Scotland, particularly the north east. In Aberdeenshire and Caithness, it was made from oatmeal or sometimes peasemeal (milled roasted dried peas): the meal is placed in a warm bowl with salt and butter, boiling water is added and it is stirred until soft. To us southern Scots it is uncooked porridge; to those in the north east brought up with brose, it is morning ambrosia. In this soup, the mussels are returned to the pan towards the end and it is served in warm bowls with a scattering of chives.

Before cooking the mussels, ensure they are all still alive by tapping any opened shells: any remaining open must be discarded. Only cook those with tightly closed shells after washing well in many changes of water and scrubbing to remove any barnacles adhering to the shell.

Serves 4

1kg mussels, well-scrubbed
300ml full-fat milk
300ml fish stock
75g fine or medium oatmeal, toasted
Chives to garnish
A swirl of cream, optional

Once the mussels are thoroughly scrubbed and washed, place in a pan with 600ml of cold water. Cover tightly and bring slowly to the boil, shaking the pan a couple of times. Allow the mussels to boil for a minute or two, or until the shells are opened, then remove and strain over a large jug.

Next, heat together the milk, fish stock and 600ml of the mussel liquor. Bring slowly to the boil, then reduce the heat to medium. Remove a ladleful of the liquid and stir into the oatmeal in a bowl, stirring well until smooth. Add this gradually to the pan, also whisking or stirring well until smooth. (If the oatmeal is still rather 'knotty', tip the mixture into a blender and whizz until smooth.) Cook gently for a couple of minutes, until the oatmeal has just cooked.

Remove the mussels from their shells and return to the pan. Reheat gently – for a minute or so – then taste and season accordingly. Serve in warm bowls with some chopped chives and a swirl of cream if you like.

Meat and Game

PEPPERCORNS

PRUNES

PARSLEY

Cock-a-Leekie

Hailed by many as Scotland's other national soup (Scotch Broth holds that accolade) it never ceases to amaze me how such a delicious soup can be made from so few ingredients. I like to serve the soup in bowls and the chicken on a separate platter (ashet) for the cook to carve at table, and the pieces then dropped into the soup as required. Alternatively, the cook can do the chopping of the flesh in the kitchen and replace it in the soup to reheat just before serving. The main thing is to avoid overcooking the chicken, otherwise it becomes tough. Traditional recipes recommend simmering for 4 hours, then serving at once. I like to cook the chicken for a far shorter time, leaving it to cool in the stock before reheating the bird either whole or in pieces. I also discard the rather slimy green parts of the leeks and replace them with the white parts of the leek, which are cooked until just done.

The prunes are essential to elevate this soup from simply a chicken and leek soup to a traditional Scottish soup. They add both sweetness and colour.

Serves 6

1 small free-range chicken (1.1–1.2kg)
6 long, thick leeks, trimmed
10–12 black peppercorns
12–16 stoned prunes
1 tablespoon chopped parsley

Place the chicken in a large saucepan. Halve and wash the leeks well and cut off the green parts. Chop these roughly and add to the pan with the peppercorns and enough water to just cover – about 2 litres. Bring slowly to the boil, then cover and simmer, with the lid on, for about 25–30 minutes. Switch off the heat, cover tightly and leave for at least an hour.

Then use a slotted spoon to remove the chicken as well as the leeks, which can be discarded. Add the chopped leek whites and the prunes and bring the broth to the boil again. Cook for about 10 minutes until just done.

If you are serving the chicken whole, return it to the soup pan for the last 5 minutes or so, to warm through. Otherwise, chop the chicken flesh into pieces and add these to the soup. Add plenty of salt and pepper to taste and serve with chopped parsley sprinkled over it.

Bawd Bree

This is the Scots name for hare soup. It has a delicious, rich, gamey taste.

My Dundonian father remembers going to his Granny Anderson's on Christmas Day for a meal of hare soup, followed by cloutie dumpling for pudding. Though the dumpling was traditional and most people in Dundee would have been eating that too, the hare soup was idiosyncratic. His granny had been in service in one of the big estates in rural Angus where game would have been served daily during the season. In Scotland the open season for brown hare is 1 October until 31 January; for mountain hare it is 1 August until 28 February.

Butchers advise washing the hare pieces in salted water, rinsing thoroughly and drying before cooking.

Serves 6

1 hare, skinned, cleaned and cut into pieces
40g seasoned flour
60g butter
2 large onions, peeled and chopped
75g unsmoked streaky bacon, chopped
3–4 carrots, peeled and chopped
2 sticks of celery, chopped
2–3 sprigs of parsley
2–3 sprigs of thyme
1.5 litres of beef stock, hot
50ml port

Dip the hare in the flour and brown it all over in 40g butter in a solid pan. (You will need to do this in batches.) Remove the hare and gently fry the onions and bacon in the remaining butter for about 10 minutes, then add the carrots and celery. Continue to cook for about 5 minutes and next add the herbs, hot stock, the hare pieces and salt and pepper. Bring to the boil, skim if necessary, cover and simmer gently for about 2 hours (an older, tougher hare will need longer – about 3 hours). Remove the hare pieces and, once it is cool enough to handle, shred the meat into small pieces. Liquidise the soup – in batches – and return to the soup pan with the meat. Stir in the port, reheat and add salt and pepper to taste. Once it is hot, check if it needs any extra port – a final splash would not go amiss.

Scotch Broth

'This is the comfortable *pot au feu* of Scotland,' wrote Meg Dods in her 1826 *The Cook and Housewife's Manual*, about Scotland's national soup. Most people enjoying a plate of broth as a starter before a main course might not see the similarities, but, served – as it was and often still is – as a soup course with the meat and freshly boiled vegetables served as a main course thereafter – it is closer to France's famous *pot au feu* than any other dish. Often tiny whole potatoes, turnips or carrots would be added with the vegetables and cooked until tender, then these would be removed to an ashet (platter) and arranged around the meat. My Dundonian family sometimes ate broth in this way (soup then the meat and vegetables) for Sunday dinner.

This recipe might provide a soup that is too bulgingly thick; if that is the case, simply add more boiling water after the initial cooking. (I like a hale and hearty soup.)

Serves 6

A piece of boiling beef (runner, thin rib or flank) – or a marrow bone – or neck of mutton or shoulder of lamb – about 700g in weight
150g dried marrowfat peas, soaked overnight
75g pearl barley, rinsed
25g parsley (including stalks) plus extra leaves, chopped, to garnish
200g carrots, peeled and finely diced
150g kail, washed and finely chopped
200g turnip (swede), peeled and finely diced
1 large onion, peeled and finely chopped

Place the meat with the soaked peas and the barley in a large pan with the stalks from the parsley. Cover with cold water, about 2.25 litres, and bring slowly to the boil. Then skim off any scum and lower to a simmer. Cover and cook for one and a half hours or until the peas are tender.

Remove the parley stalks if possible (don't worry if some remain) and add all the vegetables (with some extra boiling water, if necessary). Bring to the boil again and cook for about 15 minutes, or until tender. Add salt and pepper to taste with most of the parsley (chopped) and heat through.

To serve, remove the meat and cut into pieces. Add these to the soup and serve sprinkled with a little extra parsley. (You could, however, serve the vegetable broth first and then the beef as a main course, in which case add a few whole vegetables to the diced ones from the soup – such as tiny whole potatoes, turnips and carrots.)

Reestit Mutton Soup

Reested or reestit mutton is Shetland's cured mutton: it is salted for at least 10 days, then hung up on hooks over peat fires to dry for as long as it takes to be eaten up. After some time it looks rather like salt cod, with an ivory hue and a stiff cardboard feel. Some people have it hanging there for so long they wrap it around with newspapers to prevent the dust settling on it. The mutton is then sliced thinly – parma ham thinness – and fried with onions. Or – best of all – made into soup. Traditionally eaten with slices of the cold reested mutton on the side, the slices are also occasionally added to the soup just before serving.

Reested mutton was traditionally eaten during the winter months – originally it was a means of preserving when there was little fresh meat – and is most readily available in butchers' shops in the run-up to Christmas.

Serves 6

450g reested mutton
1 onion, peeled, chopped and cut into chunks
4–5 large carrots, peeled and cut into chunks
1 medium turnip (swede), peeled and cut into chunks
6–8 floury potatoes, peeled and cut into chunks

Place the mutton in a large pan and cover with cold water. Bring to the boil and cook for about 30 minutes, then add all the vegetables.

Return to the boil and cook, covered, until everything is tender – about 20 minutes. Remove the meat, cut off slices and put onto a plate. Serve piping hot, with the plate of sliced meat on the side.

Hotch Potch

Rather like Scotch Broth, this is somewhere between a soup and a stew. Chunky and hearty, it is a thick soup that requires only the addition of some fresh bread as accompaniment to make a main course.

The etymology of the word is interesting. Originally from the French, '*hochepot*', hotchpotch now means a dish of mixed ingredients such as a stew with vegetables. My French dictionary is more specific and indicates it is a mutton, beef or fowl ragout with turnips and chestnuts. And so my recipe is a modernised version of the old recipes, using lamb (neck and/or shoulder) instead of mutton and as many vegetables as can be crammed in. I have left out the chestnuts, although they were extremely popular in Scotland in the past.

The secret of a good hotchpotch is in the slow-cooking, in order to have tender pieces of meat and a richly flavoured broth. If you dislike a fatty taste to your broth, cook the first stage – for 2 hours – then chill. Scrape off surface fat and reheat to boiling before adding the remaining vegetables.

Serves 6

900g neck and/or shoulder of lamb (traditionally the bone is left in) chopped into very large pieces
6 carrots, peeled and left whole
600g baby turnips, peeled and left whole
1 large onion, peeled and cut into sixths or eighths
3–4 sprigs of thyme
4 large (or 8 medium) spring onions
1 small cauliflower, cut into florets
3 heaped tablespoons freshly chopped parsley

Place the meat in the base of a large heavy casserole. Top with 2 whole carrots, the whole turnips, onion and the thyme. Cover with 1.5 litres cold water, add salt and pepper and bring slowly to the boil. Skim, before covering and cooking over a very low heat for about 2 hours. (Skim again if necessary.) Then bring the mixture up to the boil, add the remaining whole carrots, the whole spring onions and the cauliflower florets. Cook over a medium heat, covered, for about 15 minutes, or until the vegetables are just cooked. Check the seasoning and stir in the parsley. Serve in deep plates or bowls, with plenty of good bread and butter on the side.

Oxtail Soup

All the old-fashioned recipes for Oxtail Soup stipulate jointing a whole oxtail yourself. I would not recommend this: those bones require serious hacking skills only possessed by a professional – i.e. the butcher. Also, traditional recipes start with the cook having to soak the oxtail in cold water for several hours. Nowadays this is unnecessary.

Old recipes insist you make the soup the day before, so that the stock solidifies and you can scrape the fat off it. Nowadays, though, when you buy ready jointed oxtail, much extraneous fat has been removed so the resulting stock is not nearly as greasy.

This soup made with cold water is not as dark brown as tinned oxtail soup of yore! For a richer and definitely darker colour, use beef stock instead of water. I

however prefer the lighter soup with the natural flavour simply of the oxtail and a good hint of garden thyme.

Serves 4–6

1 tablespoon of olive oil
800–900g oxtail, jointed
1 large onion, peeled and thinly sliced
3 carrots, peeled and sliced
3 sticks of celery, chopped
1.2 litres cold water or beef stock
A good handful of fresh thyme
100ml amontillado sherry
Worcestershire sauce

Heat the oil in a large pan then add the oxtail pieces and cook, turning once, to brown all over. Add the onion, carrots and celery and stir well. Cook gently for 5 minutes or so, then add the stock or cold water to cover and the thyme. Bring slowly to the boil and reduce to a simmer. Put a lid on the pan and cook for about 2 hours, until the meat is tender. Transfer the pieces of oxtail to a plate and remove and discard the thyme.

Shred the meat into pieces and set aside. Tip the remains of the pan – the stock and vegetables – into a liquidiser with the sherry, adding plenty of salt and pepper. Blend till smooth, then check the seasoning. Add a few shakes of Worcestershire sauce and taste again.

Return to a pan to heat up, add the shredded meat and serve piping hot.

Oeufs Files
LE CHANNEL CROSSING

Feather Fowlie

I have always loved the name of this dish: at first I assumed the Fowlie part of it was from the fact it is a chicken-based soup. However F. Marian McNeill in her *Scots Kitchen* says the name is a corruption of the French '*Oeufs Filés*', which is a light potage with strained eggs added slowly to form long 'strings' of egg. (The French word '*fil*' means thread or string.) Remember that many dishes crossed the Channel (in both directions!) during the Auld Alliance when Scotland had more trade and cultural dealings with France than it did with England, before the Union of the Crowns in 1603; even up to and after the Union of the Parliaments in 1707, many French terms continued to be used in the Scots kitchen.

I see the addition of eggs and cream to this Scots soup, however, as more like *avgolemono*, a delicious Greek soup with eggs and lemon juice beaten into a chicken soup towards the end to enrich it and make it creamy.

This recipe is, like so many others, all about having the best ingredients. Use only a free-range chicken. In both F. Marian McNeill's and Theodora Fitzgibbon's recipes, the chicken is jointed, so if you like you should joint it too. I like the simplicity of popping the chicken whole into the pot. This soup is wholesome and nourishing, ideal for a cold Scottish winter's evening.

Serves 6

25g butter
125g unsmoked streaky bacon, finely chopped
3–4 sticks of celery, finely chopped
1 onion, peeled and finely chopped
1 chicken, 1–1.2kg, whole or jointed
3 large free-range egg yolks
2 tablespoons double cream
Freshly snipped chives

Melt the butter in a large pan and fry the bacon for 2–3 minutes before adding the celery and onion. Stir well to coat in the fat and gently fry till softened – about 5 minutes.

Add the chicken (if whole, press it down so legs are not poking out of the pan!) and cover with 1.8 litres of cold water. Don't worry if the bird is not fully submerged; but if it is not, keep ladling some of the stock over the breast as it cooks. Bring to the boil, reduce to a simmer, cover with a tight lid and cook for 50 minutes for a whole bird and 40 minutes if it is jointed, then remove the bird to a platter and carve off the meat.

Push the egg yolks over a plastic sieve into a bowl (this is to avoid globby bits in the soup!) and mix them with the cream. With the soup pan now over a gentle heat, very slowly dribble in the egg and cream mixture with one hand, whisking with your other hand as you do so. Once all has been added, stir well and add salt and pepper to taste. Return the chicken meat to the pan, then serve in warm bowls with plenty of chives over the top.

Hairst Bree

Hairst Bree means Harvest Broth, and was traditionally made in the late summer when the vegetables are young and tender. I like to make this in any season, however, and you can simply vary the vegetables used. Cabbage or kail can also be used; adding some tiny new potatoes makes it more of a main course meal; and mint is an alternative to parsley at the end. In some areas, wild garlic or young nettles would also have been added.

Mutton obviously gives a stronger flavour, but whether it is lamb or mutton, the old-fashioned method of cooking the meat in water first to give instant stock is one that ensures a true, lingering, meaty taste.

The old recipes stipulated that the meat be cooked for about 45 minutes and the vegetables for a good hour; I have reduced all cooking timings so that the end result is a fresh-tasting, vibrant soup.

Serves 4

500g neck of lamb, or mutton chops
Half a turnip, peeled and diced
3 large carrots, peeled and diced
Half a large cauliflower, cut into small florets
1 lettuce heart (e.g. Romaine or Little Gem), roughly chopped
5–6 fat spring onions, trimmed and roughly chopped
A handful of peas or small broad beans
A generous handful of flat parsley, chopped

Place the meat in a large saucepan with enough cold water to cover – about 1.2 litres. Bring slowly to the boil, reduce to a simmer and cook gently, with the lid on, for 20 minutes. Then, using a slotted spoon, remove the meat to a platter. Add salt and pepper to the broth with the turnip and carrot. Cook, again with the lid on, for a further 15 minutes or until tender. Meanwhile, trim the neck of lamb or chops: remove and discard the bones and fat, slice the meat into pieces and set aside.

Add the cauliflower and cook for a further 10 minutes, then add the lettuce, spring onions and peas or beans. Cook until just tender but with the peas or beans still vivid green, about 5 minutes, adding the meat after a couple of minutes. Remove from the heat and stir in the parsley. Check the seasoning and ladle into warm bowls.

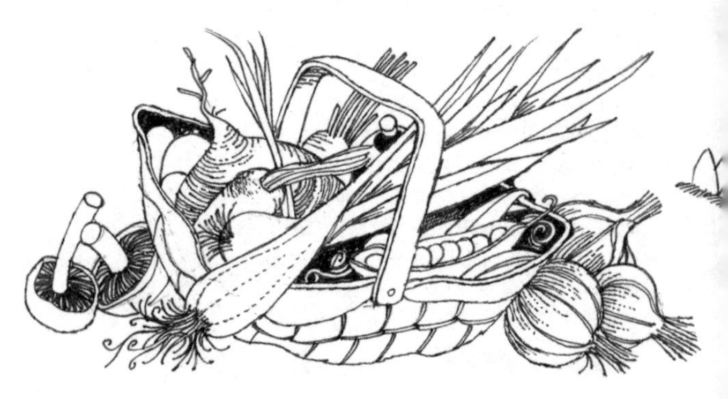

CHIVES

Ham Shank and Pea Soup

This is a delicious winter soup that is incredibly simple – and cheap – to make, and, because of its heartiness, becomes a meal in itself. The meat from the ham shank (also called hock – or hough in Scots) is shredded and served in the soup later. A good dollop of mustard – though not traditional – makes it even more special.

When I lived in the north of Finland, one of my favourite days of the week was a Thursday . . . which sounds odd until I tell you that in every public institution (schools, civil service buildings – presumably prisons), lunch was thick pea soup and then oven pancake with lingonberry jam. The soup was thick and delicious and always finished with a dollop of mustard; the mustard preferred in Finland is mild and so we tended to be generous with our spoonfuls!

Remember to start the night before as both the peas and the ham need to be soaked.

Serves 4

300g green split peas

1 ham shank, smoked or unsmoked, 600–750g

1 large onion, peeled and chopped

4 sticks of celery, chopped

Dijon mustard, optional, to serve

The night before, soak the peas in cold water. Place the ham shank in a separate bowl and cover with cold water. Leave both overnight.

Next day, drain and rinse the peas and place in a soup pan. Rinse the ham and add, with the onion and celery. Add enough cold water to cover – about 1.5 litres – and plenty of black pepper, and bring slowly to the boil. Skim off any scum, then boil rapidly for 5 minutes, reduce to a simmer and cook, lid on, for a further hour or until the meat is tender. Top up with extra boiling water every now and then, as the peas thicken as they cook.

Remove the shank and set aside. Once it is cool, shred the meat, discarding the fat. Liquidise the soup, adding salt and extra boiling water if necessary, then serve piping hot with pieces of ham and a dollop of mustard, if using.

Butter
Chicken Stock HOT

Howtowdie Soup wi' Drappit Eggs

This delicious recipe is based on one in Meg Dods' 1826 *The Cook and Housewife's Manual*, a dish of chicken surrounded by enriched cooking juices, spinach and poached eggs. The chicken is browned all over, then stewed or cooked in the oven in stock until meltingly tender. Some eggs are poached or dropped ('drappit') in the stock and these are served on spinach.

At the end of the recipe there is a comment on the dish by 'MD', suggesting you can add mushrooms, oysters or forcemeat balls. The first two would work well in this soup, the mushrooms cooked and added to the bowls with the spinach; the oysters uncooked and added to the bowl raw. These would then be warmed through with the heat of the broth ladled on top. She adds that 'a small salted tongue . . . will make a nice family dinner dish.' So slivers of boiled tongue can be added to the bowl with the chicken, spinach and shallots for added texture and flavour.

The word Howtowdie is interesting. Some references explain its etymology as being from Old French '*hutaudeau*' meaning a pullet. And in my Scots Thesaurus its meaning is 'a large young chicken for the pot, a young hen which has not begun to lay'.

Be sure to use a free-range or organic chicken whose flavour and texture will withstand the longer cooking.

Serves 4
50g butter
1 free-range chicken, giblets removed (about 1.5kg)
350g shallots
1 litre chicken stock, hot
250g young spinach, washed and lightly cooked
4 medium free-range eggs

Heat the butter in a lidded casserole (one that can go on the hob and in the oven), add the chicken and brown well all over. Peel the shallots but leave them whole. (The easiest way to peel shallots is to place them in a bowl and cover with boiling water for a minute, then drain and peel: the skin will slip off easily.) Tuck the shallots all around the bird, pour over the hot stock and season well. Cover tightly with a lid (if it is not a good seal, use foil and a lid). Place in a preheated oven (180°C/350°F/gas 4) for 1¼–1½ hours until tender and cooked through. Remove the chicken and shallots and keep the shallots warm. Carve the chicken into pieces and keep warm. Warm four soup bowls and place some chicken and shallots in each bowl, then top with some lightly cooked spinach.

Place the casserole on the hob and then, once it is gently simmering, carefully drop in the eggs, one at a time, to poach. (I like to gently draw the white around the yolk with a slotted spoon as they poach.) After a couple of minutes they should be done, so remove the pan from the heat. Taste the broth for seasoning and add salt and pepper to taste.

To serve, ladle some broth over each bowl and top with a poached egg. Grind over some black pepper and serve at once.

Chicken and Rice Soup

This is a useful dish to do on a Monday after you have made wholesome chicken stock from Sunday's roast chicken carcass. Make the stock by boiling up the carcass with half an onion or a chopped leek, a stick of celery, some black peppercorns and enough water to cover. Simmer for 30–40 minutes before straining. The addition of the rice makes this soup substantial enough to be a main course.

Though not traditional, I like a squeeze of fresh lemon juice in the soup at the last minute, just before serving.

Serves 4

1 litre good chicken stock
3 leeks, cleaned and sliced
3 sticks of celery, chopped
175g long grain rice, rinsed
Left-over cooked chicken, shredded
3 spring onions, finely chopped, *or* a handful of chopped parsley

---

Place the first four ingredients in a soup pan. Bring to the boil, then season with salt and pepper and simmer for about 20 minutes or until the rice is tender. Add the cooked chicken and check the seasoning before serving, piping hot and with chopped spring onions or parsley scattered over it.

Vegetables and Pulses

Wee Ticky Soup

My Auntie Muriel – like most other Scots women of her generation – always had a pot of soup on the go. Auntie Muriel's pot of soup sat on the cooker day in, day out, and almost invariably had things added to it. It always tasted delicious, but when anyone ever asked what was in it, she'd say, 'Oh, just a wee ticky of this and a wee ticky of that.'

You can make this soup with a variety of ingredients. The following are just suggestions; don't use too much of one thing though. Vegetables such as cauliflower or celeriac tend to overwhelm in quantity. There should be no dominant flavour, just a wholesome tasty soup.

If you want to speed up this soup, soak the split peas in cold water overnight; this means you can reduce cooking time by about 15 minutes.

Serves 4

2 handfuls of yellow split peas, rinsed
2 sticks of celery, chopped
2 leeks, trimmed and chopped
3–4 potatoes, peeled and chopped
3 carrots, peeled and chopped
1.5–1.75 litres chicken or vegetable stock
2 good handfuls of kail or cabbage, stalks removed, washed and sliced

---

First, place the split peas in a bowl and pour boiling water from a kettle over them while you prepare the vegetables. Then drain the peas and place in a pan with the next five ingredients and some ground black pepper and bring to the boil. Boil rapidly for 10 minutes, then reduce to a simmer and, with the lid on, continue to cook until the split peas are tender, 35–40 more minutes.

Add the kail (or cabbage), cook until it is tender yet still bright green – 5 minutes or so. Season with salt and extra pepper and serve piping hot.

Barley and Bean Soup

This is hearty and nourishing, a real rib-sticker of a soup. You can thin it down at the end if it is too thick for you. Add a drizzle of best green olive oil just before serving in the style of Tuscan Ribollita, although this is obviously very unScottish!

Remember to start the night before by soaking the beans.

Serves 6–8

250g dried butterbeans
200g pearl barley, rinsed
2 sticks of celery, chopped
4 carrots, peeled and chopped
3 leeks, cleaned and sliced
2.5 litres of stock (beef or vegetable)
Half a small green cabbage, sliced
Extra virgin olive oil, optional

Soak the butterbeans overnight, drain and rinse.

Tip into a pan with all the other ingredients except the cabbage and olive oil. Bring to the boil and boil rapidly for 10 minutes, reduce to a simmer and cook for about 45 minutes (or until the beans and barley are tender), then add the cabbage and continue to cook for a further 5–10 minutes. Season to taste with salt and pepper, adding a little extra boiling water if too thick. Serve piping hot, with or without a slug of best olive oil.

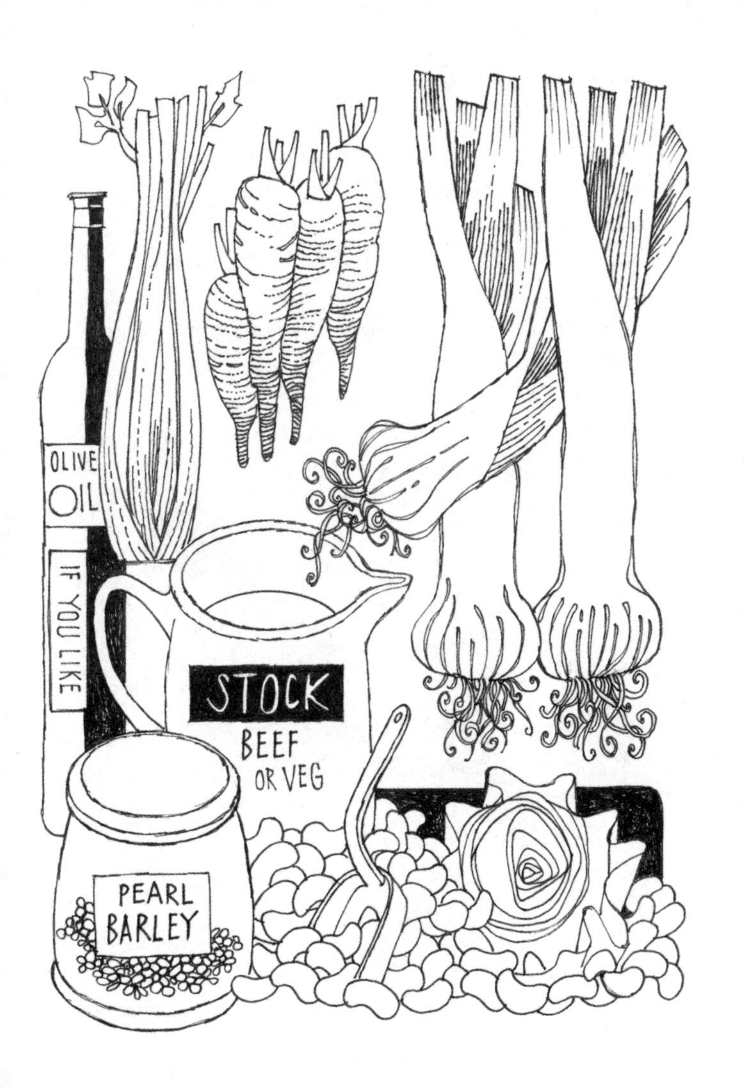
OLIVE OIL
IF YOU LIKE
STOCK
BEEF OR VEG
PEARL BARLEY

Cauliflower Cheese Soup

Cauliflower Cheese is not recognised as traditionally Scottish in the way that, say, Scotch Broth or haggis are, but it has been so much a part of most Scots' childhoods that I present it here, in soup form, with justification – and pride!

I have also made cauliflower cheese soup by simply blitzing leftover cauli cheese with hot stock – the simplest of all soup methods. But since there is seldom very much cauli cheese left over in my house, this is only an occasional possibility.

I like to add a few shakes of truffle oil – unScottish, I agree, but oh so delicious. It also elevates this humble (and very cheap) soup to something that seems to have suddenly acquired luxury status merely by the unscrewing the lid of a tiny bottle of truffle oil.

Serves 4

1 tablespoon extra virgin olive oil
1 large onion, peeled and chopped
1 large cauliflower, washed and the core and outer leaves removed, chopped
1 litre hot chicken or vegetable stock
100g grated cheese (I like mature Cheddar)
Truffle oil, optional

Heat the oil in a wide pan, then add the onion and sauté for a few minutes before adding the cauliflower. Cook over a medium heat for a few minutes until it is just beginning to acquire a nice golden hue. Stir often.

Add the hot stock, bring to the boil and then simmer, lid on, for about 15 minutes or until the vegetables are tender. Remove a ladle of the hot stock (avoid the veg) and mix with the cheese in a bowl, until it is molten. Whizz or blitz contents of pan, then stir cheese mixture back into the soup; continue stirring until melted throughout. Season well with salt and pepper to taste.

To serve, ladle into warm bowls and shake over a few drops of truffle oil just before serving.

Kail Soup with Oatmeal

This hardy winter vegetable was grown in most regions of Scotland, not only for its ability to withstand severe cold and frost, but also because, as is now recognised, it is a bit of a superstar nutritionally: packed with calcium, potassium, iron, vitamins A and C and high in fibre. So commonplace was kail as a vegetable, the word kail (the Scots spelling for kail) had other meanings. To be asked to take kail was an invitation for a meal. And the kail-yard was the term for the kitchen garden where vegetables were grown. F. Marian MacNeill, in her description of an average Scottish kitchen in a 'but-and-ben' (two-roomed cottage) or croft wrote of the kail-pot, a round iron pot with three legs to stand it over the peat fire. In the kail-pot, as well as morning porridge, the midday broth or brose was made. My mother remembers broth referred to in her childhood as simply 'kail' because of the vegetable in the soup.

Many broths in Scotland thickened with oatmeal are known as brose. Kail brose is typical of many regions of Scotland where curly kail was widely grown. Apart from broths and soups, it was served on its own, with butter and milk added when available. Dr Samuel Johnson remarked in his 1775 *A Journey to the Western Islands of Scotland* that 'when they [the Scots] had not kail, they probably had nothing.'

Kail brose was eaten in some regions in a way similar to the traditional ritual of porridge eating that my parents grew up with. The milk and porridge were in separate bowls and a spoonful of porridge was then dipped into the bowl of milk; it kept the porridge as hot as possible which, for those pre-central heating days, would have been not only welcome, but essential. For the brose, toasted oatmeal would be placed in each bowl with a pinch of salt, then a ladleful of boiling beef broth stirred in and the puréed kail served separately. A spoonful of kail was dipped into the broth and the two eaten together.

At the onset of spring, nettles would often be substituted in the brose recipe, but a lighter chicken stock was more likely to be used for the less robust flavour of nettles.

A traditional kail brose used beef stock: classically it was made by boiling an ox head, cow heel or marrow bone to make good fatty stock, then the kail cooked in this liquid with some toasted oatmeal stirred in towards the end to thicken and flavour. Lady Clark of Tillypronie advocated a half teacupful of warmed cream just before serving. And although this might sound extravagant, it is not impossible that some cottages and crofts would have cream to spare after their cottage cheese – crowdie – was made.

Serves 4

300g kail, stalks stripped off, washed and roughly chopped
1.2 litres beef or vegetable stock, hot
1 medium onion, peeled and chopped
50g fine or medium oatmeal

Place most of the kail (setting aside a large handful of leaves) in a large pan with the hot stock and onion. Bring to the boil, cover and cook over a medium heat, stirring once, for 10 minutes or until the kail is just tender.

Meanwhile, place the oatmeal on a sheet of foil and place under a preheated grill for 3–4 minutes, shaking often to prevent burning, until toasted and pale golden.

Tip the soup into a blender or liquidiser with the remaining kail and blend. (You will need to do this in two batches.)

Return the soup to the pan and gradually stir in the oatmeal as you cook over a medium heat. Add 1 level teaspoon of salt and plenty of freshly milled pepper. Cook, stirring to avoid lumps of oatmeal, for 4–5 minutes or until thickened. Serve with thick oatcakes.

Kail and Barley Soup

This is a hearty, thick soup that is perfect on a cold winter's day. I think turnip works well with kail and barley, but you could substitute carrots or parsnips for a change.

Serves 6

200g pearl barley, rinsed
2 leeks
Half a medium turnip (neep), peeled and diced
2 litres beef or vegetable stock
250g kail, stalks stripped off, washed and roughly chopped

Place the barley, leeks and turnip in a large soup pan with the stock. Bring to the boil and boil rapidly for 10 minutes, then reduce to a simmer, with the lid on, for a further 40 minutes or so, until the barley is tender. Add plenty of salt and pepper, then add the kail and continue to cook for 8–10 minutes until the kail is still green, but tender. Add some more hot water if it is too thick. Check the seasoning and serve piping hot.

Butterbean Soup

Butterbeans were often used in the Scots kitchen, mainly in soups but also to enrich and thicken stews.

Though not traditional, I like to add a sprig or two of rosemary to enhance the flavour of this soup. A sprinkling of grated cheese makes it even more delicious: I would recommend one of Scotland's great cheddar-style cheeses such as Loch Arthur or Mull.

Serves 4–6

350g dried butterbeans
2 tablespoons olive oil
1 large onion, peeled and chopped
3 garlic cloves, peeled and chopped
1.2 litres vegetable stock
2 thick sprigs of rosemary
50g coarsely grated Scottish farmhouse cheddar, optional

Soak the beans overnight, then drain and rinse. Heat the olive oil in a saucepan and gently fry the onion and garlic for 10 minutes. Add the beans, hot stock, rosemary and some black pepper (no salt yet). Bring to the boil, cover and simmer gently for about 1 hour or until the beans are tender.

Remove the rosemary (and try to retrieve most of the spiny leaves which will have dropped off) then purée about half the soup, leaving some beans whole. Or just mash with a potato masher, again leaving some beans whole. Now add salt – and pepper if necessary – according to taste.

To serve, ladle into warm bowls and top with some cheese, if using.

Tattie Soup

Although Tattie Soup is traditionally made with mutton stock, my recipe uses chicken stock which I reckon more people are likely to have at home. This is a very simple recipe and relies on using a really good stock, from a free-range/organic chicken. I am usually happy to fling in an organic stock cube for some recipes, but this soup tastes much better with home-made stock.

Serves 6

1.2 litres good chicken stock
1kg potatoes (unpeeled weight), peeled
1 large onion, peeled
3–4 carrots, peeled
Chopped chives or parsley

Bring the stock to the boil in a large saucepan. Chop the vegetables into similarly sized dice and add them to the pan, with some salt and pepper. Cover and cook over a medium heat for 25–30 minutes until the vegetables are all tender. Taste and check the seasoning.

Sprinkle each soup bowl with some chopped chives or parsley to serve.

Dulse Soup (using fresh seaweed)

Dulse – *Palmaria palmata* – is prolific around the coast of Scotland, and this simple, traditional soup uses fresh dulse. When harvesting seaweed, ensure it is from clean water and that there is no sewage plant just around the bay!

It is surprising how much flavour is in a bowl of this soup, for there is no stock used. But the pure flavour of the sea comes through in a pleasing way.

There is another Hebridean seaweed soup made with either dulse or sloke (laver in Wales, nori in Japan): a good handful or two is stewed with some milk, then flavoured with pepper, butter and lemon juice or vinegar.

Dried dulse can also be used for this soup; rinse and soak in warm water for 5–10 minutes first.

Serves 4–6

About 200g freshly picked dulse, well washed (or 50g dried dulse)
4 large potatoes, peeled and chopped
2 onions, peeled and chopped
Thick/coarse oatcakes, to serve

Place everything in a large saucepan and cover with water. Bring to the boil, then simmer for about 10 minutes until the potatoes are tender. Liquidise and add salt and pepper to taste. Serve piping hot, topped with roughly crumbled oatcakes.

Palmaria Palmata

Dulse and Oatmeal Soup (using dried seaweed)

This recipe can be made any time, not just after a day's beachcombing, as it uses dried dulse. I add the fresh parsley to improve the colour of the soup, which otherwise would be sludge brown!

It is delicious topped with flakes of hot-smoked salmon or Arbroath smokies.

Serves 4

40g dried dulse, rinsed and then soaked in warm water for 5–10 minutes
2 large potatoes, peeled and diced
1 large leek, trimmed and chopped
25g medium oatmeal
40g fresh parsley
Fillet of hot-smoked salmon or 1 small Arbroath smokie and extra-virgin olive oil, to serve

---

Drain the dulse and place in a pan with the potatoes, leeks and about 800ml cold water. Season, bring to the boil, cover and simmer for about 10 minutes. Mix the oatmeal in a cup with about 3 tablespoons of the cooking liquor, then gradually stir this into the soup, stirring well. (Don't worry if lumps form, as it is all about to be blitzed.) Cook gently for 5 minutes, then tip everything into a food mixer or blender (in batches) with the parsley. Check the seasoning and return to the pan.

Reheat and serve in warm bowls. Flake the salmon or smokies, if using, and scatter on top, drizzle over some olive oil and serve.

A and E
Bashed Neep Clinic
DID YOU GET A GOOD LOOK AT THE COOK?
POLICE

Turnip Soup

What is known as turnip all over Scotland is known as swede elsewhere in the UK. Just to confuse things, neeps is the word most often used for turnip in parts of Scotland and especially when haggis is eaten: champit tatties and bashed neeps are its traditional bedfellows!

This turnip soup is simple yet very tasty indeed. The idea of adding fresh ginger I got from chef Shirley Spear's delicious Neep Bree which she serves with warm cheese scones.

In Aberdeenshire, Neep Bree was traditionally made from turnips and a marrowbone, all thickened with oatmeal or barley and enriched with butter.

Serves 4–5

1 large turnip, peeled and diced
1 onion, peeled and chopped
1 leek, cleaned and sliced
3 carrots, peeled and chopped
1 knob of root ginger, peeled and finely diced
1.3–1.4 litres chicken or vegetable stock
Chopped parsley or chives, to serve

Place the first six ingredients in a large soup pan with salt and pepper. Bring to the boil and cook, lid on, for 45–50 minutes or until the vegetables are tender. Liquidise in a blender, adding a little extra boiling water if necessary to thin it down. Serve piping hot with some parsley or chives.

Carrot Soup

Carrots are ubiquitous in Scotland, a few added to everything from soups and stews to cloutie dumplings and cake. Sometimes it is good to make a tasty soup based almost solely on carrots, for their wonderful flavour – and colour!

Serves 4–5

25g butter
2 leeks, cleaned and sliced thinly
500g carrots, peeled and sliced
1.2 litres chicken or vegetable stock, hot
25g fine or medium oatmeal
3 tablespoons milk
A good handful of chopped parsley or a fine sprinkling of finely chopped tarragon

---

Melt the butter over a moderate heat, add the leeks and gently fry for 5 minutes. Add the carrots and fry for a further 5 minutes, stirring.

Add the hot stock and some salt and pepper. Bring to the boil and simmer for about 20 minutes or until the vegetables are tender.

Meanwhile, soak the oatmeal in the milk for 15–20 minutes, adding this mixture to the soup after the initial 20 minutes of simmering, and continue to cook, stirring regularly, for another 15 minutes. Tip into a blender or liquidiser and liquidise, checking the seasoning as you blend.

Serve piping hot, with some parsley or tarragon sprinkled on top.

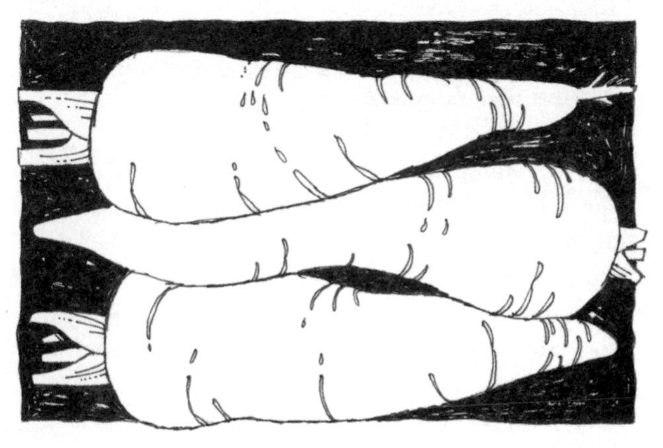

Lentil Soup

Lentil soup was a classic when I was growing up, part of everyone's mum's repertoire. It is also one of the most versatile of soups. This one is made from chicken stock, but you can use vegetable or ham stock. I like to add a knob of root ginger for added zing. You might not think this sounds very Scottish, but in fact there is reference to a dinner taken on Mull in 1784 by B. Faujas de St Fond that included roast beef with ginger pickled in vinegar. So ginger is certainly not an exotic newcomer. It tastes delicious in this, the easiest of soups.

Serves 4–5

250g red lentils, rinsed well
3 carrots, peeled and chopped
1 onion, peeled and chopped
2 sticks of celery, chopped
A good knob of root ginger, peeled and finely chopped, optional
1.2 litres chicken or vegetable stock

Place everything in a soup pan with ground black pepper. Bring to the boil, stir and boil rapidly for 10 minutes before reducing to a simmer and cooking, lid on, for a further 20 minutes or so. Tip into a liquidiser and blitz until smooth, seasoning to taste with salt. You can also mash everything together for a rougher texture, but the ginger is best puréed, otherwise you might have stringy fibres in your soup.

Lentil Soup with Bacon

Thick and wholesome, this is another variation on basic lentil soup. The bacon gives a good depth of flavour. If you like it chunky, then leave out the liquidising. You could also mash with a potato masher so you have some smooth, some chunky. This is great served with crisply grilled rashers of bacon snipped on top.

Serves 6

1 tablespoon olive oil
6–8 rashers streaky bacon, smoked or unsmoked, snipped into pieces
3 carrots, peeled and chopped
3 sticks of celery, chopped
1 onion, peeled and chopped
250g red lentils, rinsed
1.2 litres ham or chicken stock

Heat the oil in a pan, add the bacon and fry gently until cooked, then add the carrots, celery and onion. Fry gently for 3–4 minutes, stirring, until coated in fat.

Add the lentils and the stock and bring to the boil. Boil rapidly for 5 minutes, reduce to a simmer and cook, lid on, for about half an hour or until the vegetables and lentils are tender. Add salt and pepper to taste and liquidise in batches before serving, piping hot.

Nettle and Potato Soup (Traditional)

This is a traditional recipe but is also very versatile. If you don't find enough nettles, you can substitute some spinach or watercress.

When you pick nettles, I need hardly tell you that you will require rubber gloves and scissors (and welly boots unless you have long trousers). Only remove the tops and upper leaves and do not pick from plants that are in flower. Obviously pick as far away from the roadside as possible.

Once you are home (don't forget to don gloves again) remove the tender leaves from the stems, which are too fibrous to eat.

And just in case you are wondering, once they are cooked, the sting disappears immediately; all you are left with is a wonderful, rich yet sharp flavour not unlike sorrel.

Serves 6

About 250g (1 supermarket carrier bag) of young nettles
4–5 large potatoes, peeled and chopped into small dice
1 onion, peeled and finely chopped
1.2 litres chicken or vegetable stock, hot
A couple of tablespoons of double cream, optional

First put on your rubber gloves again and remove the leaves from their stalks. (Discard the stalks.) Put the leaves in a large colander and wash thoroughly, in several changes of water.

Place them in a large pan with the other ingredients and bring to the boil. Season with salt and pepper and simmer, lid on, until the vegetables are tender – 10–15 minutes. Then liquidise and adjust the seasoning. Serve piping hot, perhaps with a drizzle of cream.

Nettle Soup (Modern)

This is a more modern version of nettle soup and is delicious served with a hard-boiled egg and a drizzle of good olive oil floating on top.

Just like sorrel or spinach, nettles cook very quickly; in order to retain their vivid colour, therefore, I use the following method (which also means you do not have to make the soup the minute you get them home, for the resulting purée will last in the fridge for 2–3 days).

My method involves first blanching the leaves, then making a purée with olive oil and a little parmesan. This can then be refrigerated until used in the soup.

Serves 6

About 250g (1 supermarket carrier bag) of young nettles
Olive oil
2 heaped tablespoons of freshly grated parmesan cheese
3 large potatoes, peeled and chopped
1 large onion, peeled and chopped
2 sticks of celery, chopped
1.2 litres chicken or vegetable stock
3 large free-range eggs, hard-boiled, optional

First put on your rubber gloves again and remove the leaves from their stalks. (Discard the stalks.) Put the leaves in a large colander and wash thoroughly, in several changes of water.

Bring a large pan of water to the boil then, once it is boiling, drop in all the nettles. When it has returned to the boil, blanch the nettles for 1 minute, tip into the colander and refresh under a cold running tap. Drain really well (squeezing by hand and patting dry on kitchen paper) and pop into a small food processor. Add the parmesan and enough oil to make a thick purée – 6–8 tablespoons. Put into a bowl, cover and refrigerate for 2–3 days if necessary.

When you are ready to make the soup, place the potatoes in a pan with the onion, celery and stock. Bring to the boil and cook until the vegetables are tender. Then remove from the heat and add the nettle purée. Blend together in a blender or liquidiser and add salt and pepper to taste. Add a little extra boiling water if it is too thick. If you have to reheat, try not to boil or the lovely bright green colour will fade.

To serve, ladle into wide soup bowls. Peel and halve the hard-boiled eggs and place one in the middle of each bowl. Grind over some black pepper, drizzle over some oil and serve.

Clapshot Soup

Clapshot is a wonderful yet simple dish from Orkney and, as with so many regional dishes, there are several local variations. Sometimes the turnips are cooked in milk, which makes it even creamier; but if you do this I advise you to use a very deep saucepan and keep the heat low once it has come to the boil, otherwise the milk boils over easily. The minute you turn your back, the milk will boil up and all over your newly cleaned cooker: beware!

Sometimes a peeled, chopped onion is added to the potatoes as they cook for extra flavour. The basic recipe, however, is a mixture of potatoes and turnip (neeps) mashed together with plenty of good butter and a generous grinding of black pepper; Orkney's dairy produce is superb and the local butter, milk, cream and cheese abundant.

On Orkney, they are very particular about using winter neeps for clapshot if possible, as they are drier and so the clapshot is not watery at all. Also, in order to retain as much of the turnip's inherent sweetness, the best are those that have been in the ground through a hard frost.

This soup version of clapshot is delicious served with beremeal bannocks spread thickly with butter.

Serves 4

1 litre chicken or vegetable stock
500g potatoes (peeled weight), peeled and chopped
500g turnip (peeled weight), peeled and chopped
1 large carrot, peeled and chopped
1 onion, peeled and chopped

Bring the stock to the boil in a large saucepan, then add the vegetables and some salt and pepper. Once it boils, lower to a simmer, cover and cook for about 25 minutes or until the vegetables are tender, liquidise and check the seasoning.

Ladle into warm bowls to serve.

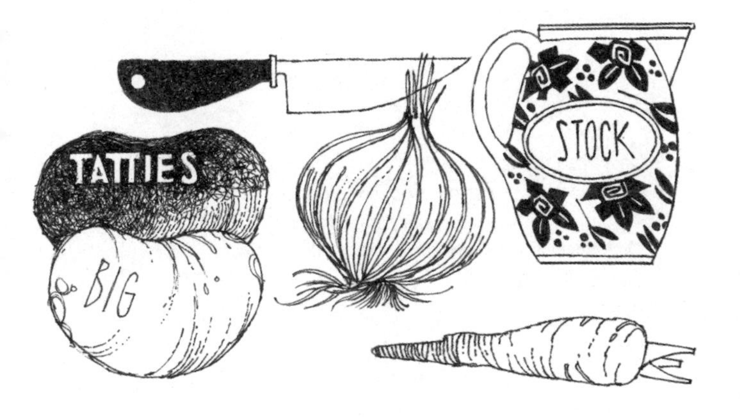

Mushroom Soup

Traditionally mushroom soup would have been made only in autumn in Scotland, when wild mushrooms such as chanterelles, ceps and puffballs were foraged in woodlands. These days, however, it can be made at any time of year because of the availability of dried wild mushrooms. But if you happen to be picking wild mushrooms then it is even more sublime. I like it best made with fresh wild chanterelles (available in the woodlands of Scotland from the end of July until the first frosts of winter) or with dried ceps (porcini). The mushroom flavour is enhanced by the addition of the fresh cultivated mushrooms.

Serves 6

250–300g fresh wild mushrooms or 50g dried wild mushrooms
250ml dry sherry or white wine
50g butter
1 onion, peeled and chopped
3 garlic cloves, peeled and chopped, optional
450g button or chestnut mushrooms, sliced
750ml chicken or vegetable stock, hot
150ml double cream
Chopped flat parsley

If using fresh mushrooms, clean them thoroughly by cutting off any root tips and cleaning with a soft brush. Slice if very large. If using dried mushrooms, rinse and

soak in the sherry or wine for about 30 minutes.
Melt the butter in a large saucepan and gently fry the onion (and garlic if using) for about 10 minutes, then add the mushrooms (if dried, drained of their liquor, which should be saved; if using fresh, add the wild and also the cultivated ones).

Stir well to coat in the fat and cook for a couple of minutes, then add the soaking liquor from the dried mushrooms, or, if using fresh, add the sherry or wine. Stir, then cook over a high heat until the liquid has evaporated. Now add the stock, salt and pepper, and bring to the boil. Cover and simmer for about 15 minutes or until tender.

Liquidise in batches and return to the pan. Reheat gently, add the cream and stir well, then check the seasoning and serve in warm bowls, topped with a scattering of chopped parsley.

Peas

Monday Soup

This could also be called Boxing Day Soup: it is the soup made from the stock from yesterday's roast chicken or turkey, and with leftover cooked vegetables thrown in. Just like Wee Ticky Soup, this is very variable, and though I have given a recipe, you can just add what you have left over. One word of caution, though: do not use too much of one thing as that one flavour can tend to dominate. Also, if it's Christmas Day leftovers, don't overdo the brussels sprouts; their flavour – and smell – is all-pervasive! I like to add fresh baby spinach at the end while blending, to liven up the flavour and introduce a fresh taste.

By the way, I have not mentioned leftover roast potatoes because – well, there never are any left over, are there?

Serves 6

1 roast chicken carcass, stripped of meat
A few black peppercorns
1 leek or half a peeled onion, roughly chopped
1 bay leaf
Leftover cooked broccoli/peas/cabbage/sprouts, 2–3 heaped tablespoons of each
Leftover mashed potatoes/cauliflower cheese, 3–4 heaped tablespoons of each
2–3 tablespoons of leftover gravy
A handful of young spinach leaves

First make the stock: place the carcass in a large pan with the peppercorns, leek or onion and bay leaf. Cover with cold water (about 800ml) and bring slowly to the boil, reduce to a simmer and simmer with the lid on for 30–40 minutes. Then strain over a wide jug. Discard the carcass and tip the stock into a food processor or blender with the other ingredients. Blend, then check the seasoning. Depending how much, say, mashed potato or other thickening vegetable such as cauliflower cheese you are using, the soup might be too thick. In this case, just add a little boiling water. Reheat and serve piping hot, with leftover cooked chicken if you like.

Tattie and Leek Soup

This is another simple soup, but one that also benefits from the best quality of ingredients, and preferably home-made stock.

Serves 4
1 litre vegetable stock
1 kg potatoes (unpeeled weight), peeled
4 fat leeks, cleaned
Double cream, optional

Bring the stock to the boil in a large saucepan.

Chop the potatoes and leeks into similarly sized slices and add, with some salt and pepper. Cover and cook over a medium heat for 20–25 minutes until the vegetables are all tender. Taste and check the seasoning. Mash with a potato masher so there is still some texture to the soup, then serve with a swirl of cream if you like.

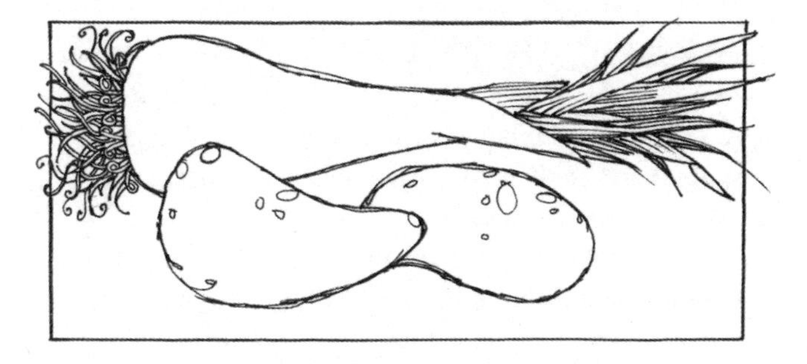

Split Pea and Carrot Soup

This is yet another ridiculously easy soup that requires only peeling and chopping, then boiling and simmering. Try to remember to soak the split peas overnight; but if you forget, don't worry. Do as I suggest for Wee Ticky Soup: place the split peas in a bowl and cover with boiling water from the kettle while you prepare the vegetables. Then drain and continue as indicated here. Although it is by no means traditional, I like to throw a handful or two of young spinach leaves into the liquidiser as I am blending the soup for added colour and taste.

Serves 6

200g yellow split peas, soaked overnight
800g carrots, peeled and chopped
1 onion, peeled and chopped
3 sticks of celery, chopped
1.8 litres ham stock
A couple of handfuls of young spinach, optional

Drain the peas, rinse and place in a pan with the remaining ingredients (except for the spinach) and bring to the boil. Boil rapidly for 10 minutes, then reduce to a simmer and cook, lid on, for about 30–35 minutes, or until the peas are tender.

Season to taste with salt and pepper, ladle into a liquidiser and blend in batches until smooth, adding the spinach if you like. Serve piping hot.